Contents

Before You Read:
Get Ready!

When you think about the United States, maybe you think of sunny California or busy New York or the farms of Kansas. This book is about Alaska – one of the 50 states in the USA, but very different from the other 49!

Words to Know

Look at the pictures. Then complete the sentences below with the correct words.

ice

tent

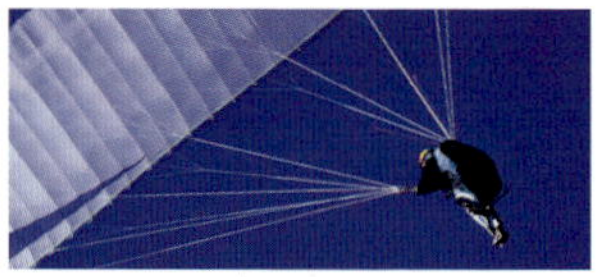
paragliding

forest

island

snow storm

1. A lot of trees in one place is called a(n) ______________________.
2. You can fly like a bird when you go ______________________.
3. A(n) ______________________ is a kind of house. You sleep in it when you are outside.
4. A(n) ______________________ is when there is a lot of snow and wind at the same time.
5. ______________________ is very cold and hard.
6. A(n) ______________________ has water all around it.

Cambridge Discovery Education™

INTERACTIVE READERS

Series editor: Bob Hastings

ALASKA

WILD AND FREE

A1+

Nic Harris

CAMBRIDGE UNIVERSITY PRESS

Discovery EDUCATION

CAMBRIDGE UNIVERSITY PRESS
Cambridge, New York, Melbourne, Madrid, Cape Town,
Singapore, São Paulo, Delhi, Mexico City

Cambridge University Press
32 Avenue of the Americas, New York, NY 10013-2473, USA

www.cambridge.org
Information on this title: www.cambridge.org/9781107674646

First published 2014

Printed in Hong Kong, China, by Golden Cup Printing Company Limited

A catalog record for this publication is available from the British Library.

Library of Congress Cataloging-in-Publication Data

Harris, Nicholas, 1956-
Alaska : wild and free / Nic Harris.
pages cm. -- (Cambridge discovery interactive readers)
ISBN 978-1-107-67464-6 (pbk. : alk. paper)
1. Alaska--Juvenile literature. 2. English language--Textbooks for foreign speakers. 3. Readers (Elementary) I. Title.

F904.3.H37 2013
979.8--dc23

2013023895

ISBN 978-1-107-67464-6

Additional resources for this publication at www.cambridge.org

Layout services, art direction, book design, and photo research: Q2ABillSMITH GROUP
Editorial services: Hyphen S.A.
Audio production: CityVox, New York
Video production: Q2ABillSMITH GROUP

Words to Know

Read the paragraph. Use the correct highlighted words to complete the definitions below.

Many tourists visit Alaska every year. They come from all over the world. It is a very popular place to go. But you must take a warm coat and a warm hat with you because the weather is very, very cold in the winter. In some places it is –20°C to –30°C. That's freezing! Some people come to Alaska to do sports. People come to climb high places. Many try to go to the top of a very tall mountain, Mount McKinley. It is dangerous. People die every year trying to climb it.

1. ______________________: very cold
2. ______________________: people who visit a place for fun
3. ______________________: not safe
4. ______________________: liked by many people
5. ______________________: go up something
6. ______________________: a very high place

CHAPTER 1

Welcome to Alaska

WHERE IS ALASKA? HOW BIG IS IT? WHO LIVES THERE?

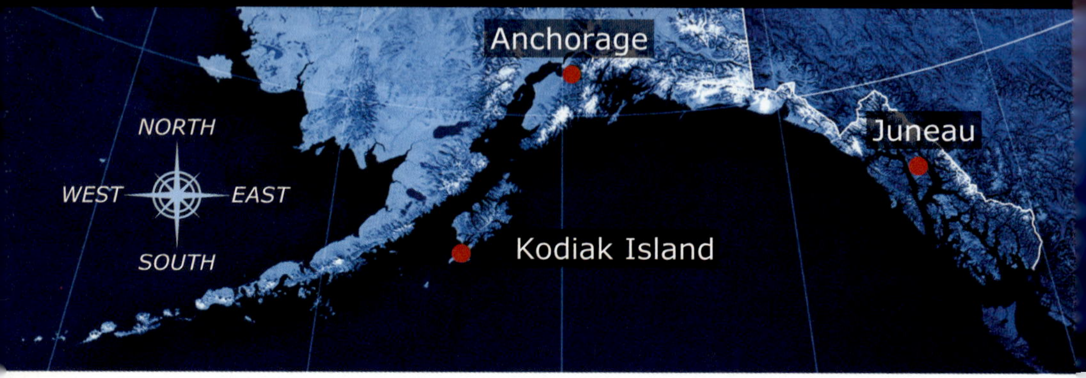

Eskimos first lived in Alaska more than 7,000 years ago. Today, about 16% of all Alaskans are Eskimos. These people are really three groups: the Inupiaq, the Yupik, and the Alutiiq. These groups are not very different, but they speak different languages.

Alaska was a part of Russia for a long time. Then in 1867, the United States bought it from Russia for $7.2 million. Many people thought this was too much money. But in the late 1840s, the Americans found gold in Alaska. Then in 1901, they found some oil[1] there. Later, in the 1950s, they found lots of oil.

Alaska is a very big place. It's the biggest state – more than twice as big as Texas, the next biggest state. But not many people live there. Over 8 million people live in New York City, but only 730,000 live in all of Alaska. And about half of them live in the city of Anchorage.

Alaska has many mountains and **glaciers**. A glacier is like a river of ice. The Matanuska glacier is one of the most beautiful.

The winters are freezing with a lot of snow storms. In winter it is also very dark because there is no sun in the far northern part of the state, and in other areas it comes out for only two to seven hours every day.

[1] **oil:** It is black. A car needs oil to make it work.

APPLY

Do people speak different languages where you live? Is the place where you live bigger or smaller than Anchorage?

CHAPTER 2

A Kodiak bear

Visit Kodiak Island

THERE IS A LOT OF OUTDOOR FUN ON KODIAK ISLAND.

Kodiak Island is in the southern part of Alaska. It is the second largest island in the United States, but it has less than 160 kilometers of roads. There are lots of high mountains, green forests, rivers, and **lakes**. About 30,000 visitors come to Kodiak every year. They come to climb mountains, catch fish, watch whales jump in the sea, and go **camping**. Bear watching is also very popular.

A whale

The island gets its name from the big Kodiak bear. There are over 3,500 of these wonderful[2] animals living in the forests. But you must be very quiet if you want to see one!

[2]**wonderful:** something very good and interesting

About 13,000 people live on Kodiak Island all year, and half of them live in Kodiak City. The others live in small villages by the sea. The Alutiiq people were the first to live on the island. They came 7,500 years ago and they stayed.

Today, about 17 percent of all the people on Kodiak Island are Alutiiqs. They speak English and Alutiiq. In 2010 only 50 people spoke the Alutiiq language! But now schools are teaching the language because they don't want it to die.

The most important businesses here are fishing and **tourism**. There are seven hotels, 17 places to eat, and many shops in Kodiak city. The shops sell things made on the island.

Video Quest

The Kodiak Bear

Watch the video to learn more about the Kodiak bear. How tall is a Kodiak bear? How much food can one eat in a day?

CHAPTER 3

Enjoy Outside Sports

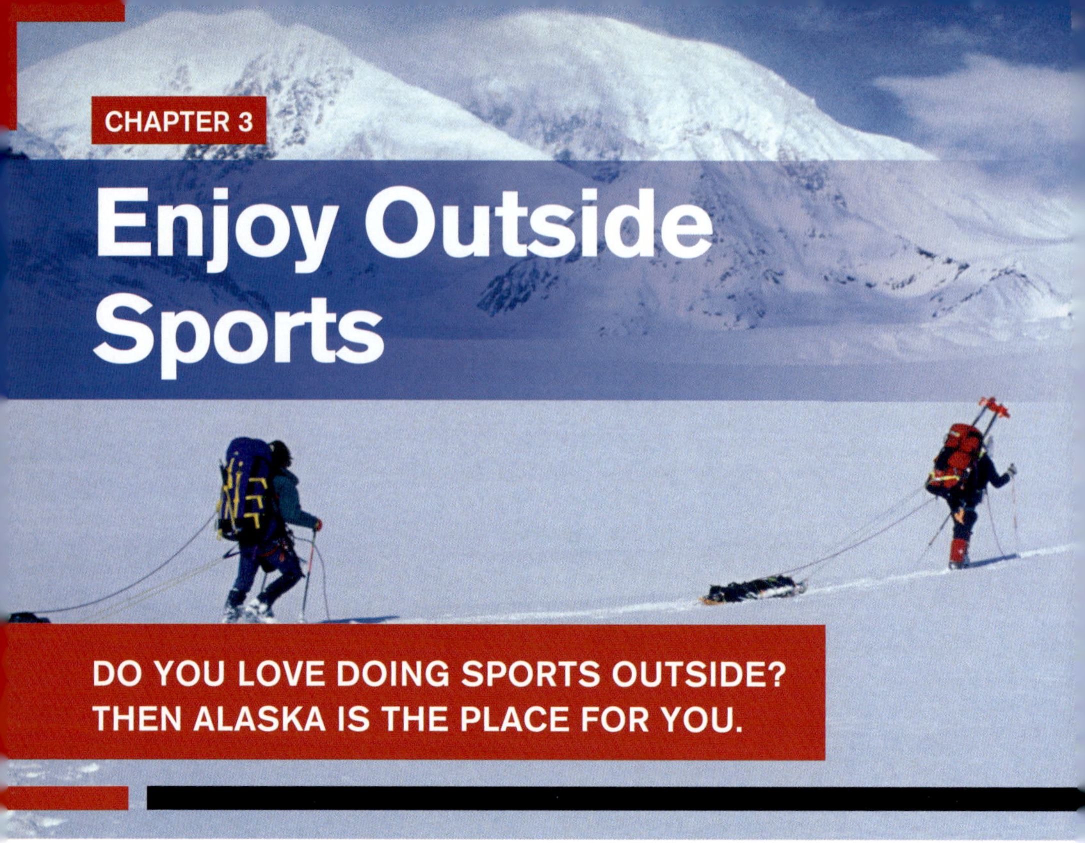

DO YOU LOVE DOING SPORTS OUTSIDE? THEN ALASKA IS THE PLACE FOR YOU.

Many **tourists** come to Alaska to enjoy walking outside in the clean, cold air. And they come to do extreme sports – sports that are exciting but also **dangerous**.

Some people come to Alaska to climb Mount McKinley in Denali National Park. This mountain is 6,194 meters high, the highest in North America.

It isn't easy to climb to the top of Mount McKinley. It takes about three weeks! It's really cold when you get to the top, so most people stay there for only a short time. You need very warm clothes. And you must be careful.[3]

[3] **be careful:** do something safely

Video Quest

Paragliding Over a Glacier

Watch this video to learn about glaciers. How many glaciers can you see from Mount Muir? How far can some glaciers travel in a day?

Between 1932 and 2012, 120 climbers died on the mountain. In June 2012, four Japanese climbers died in an **avalanche**.

Whitewater rafting is also a popular sport. The Nenana River, also in Denali National Park, is very fast in some places.

Whitewater rafting is an extreme sport.

Mount Alyeska is a good place to go paragliding. Don't worry if you don't know how to paraglide. A teacher goes on the paraglider with you so you can enjoy the beautiful mountain and forests below you.

Skiing is popular in Alaska. There is a lot of snow and there are many good places to ski. Eagle Crest, only 20 kilometers from the state capital,[4] Juneau, is an excellent mountain for skiing.

There are many other interesting things to do in Alaska. Some of these are less exciting than paragliding or whitewater rafting, but they are great fun:

- look for gold in the rivers in the Kenai Peninsula
- fly over the glaciers in a plane or a helicopter
- visit the Sea Life Center in Seward. You can see wonderful sea animals only a meter from where you are standing.

[4] **capital:** the most important city in a country or state

Some people enjoy traveling across Alaska as well. In 2010, Andrew Skurka traveled 7,600 kilometers across Alaska and the Yukon in 176 days. That's 43 kilometers a day! Most of the time he walked. He used six pairs of boots! But he also went on rivers on a raft, and he skied, too. He slept in a tent.

When Andrew skied in Denali Park, he was very worried about avalanches and snow storms. He didn't see any avalanches, but one night, there was a really bad storm and his tent blew away! Andrew has traveled 48,000 kilometers in his life, and he doesn't want to stop. When he isn't working, he writes books about his travels.

Eagle Crest is a good place for skiing.

CHAPTER 4

The Iditarod

IN THE PAST, ALASKANS NEEDED TO USE DOGS AND SLEDS TO TRAVEL. NOW THEY DON'T. BUT IN 1973, A DOGSLED RACE BEGAN, THE IDITAROD.

The Iditarod is a really hard race. The dogsled teams have to travel about 1,600 kilometers, from Anchorage to Nome. And the weather can be very bad, with freezing **temperatures** of –20°C and dangerous snow storms.

Each team has one person, called a musher, and 12 to 20 dogs. The mushers have to think about many things. When is the best time to travel, at night or in the day? What clothes are best to wear? What food is best for the dogs? When is the best time to put the boots on the dogs? If the dogs don't wear boots, the ice can cut their feet.

It usually takes 10 to 15 days to finish the Iditarod. The team that gets to Nome first **wins**! John Baker did the Iditarod in the fastest time in 2011 – 8 days and 19 hours. Carl Huntington did the slowest time in 1974 – 20 days and 15 hours.

The Iditarod is very popular. It's an important part of Alaskan life. Before the race starts, there's a big party in Anchorage. Then, thousands of people watch the race. Many more people follow it for days on TV, the Internet, or in newspapers.

In the first Iditarod there were 34 teams. Now every year in March about 55 teams do the race. Why is it so popular? Maybe because the winner gets a lot of money – about $50,000!

EVALUATE

Can you think of any other sports that use animals? Do you think it is a good thing to use animals in sports?

A musher with her dogs and sled

CHAPTER 5

Green Tourism in Alaska

TOURISTS CAN BE VERY GOOD FOR COUNTRIES. BUT TOURISTS CAN ALSO BRING PROBLEMS.

Some people leave trash like this in forests.

Tourists spend a lot of money. They stay at hotels, eat in restaurants, and buy things in shops. This is good for Alaska and its people. But a lot of people in one place can make a lot of noise. And that can be difficult for Alaska's animals. And tourists leave trash in the forests and rivers, and in the sea. Animals and fish can eat this trash and get sick.

The people at the Alaskan tourist office[5] want the state to stay clean. They want the animals to be safe and to live their normal lives. This is why they want people to do "green tourism."

[5]**office:** a room where people work

Video Quest

A Hotter World

Watch this video to learn more about temperature change. How long is the Davidson Glacier? How long was it at one time? Why is the ice **melting**?

Green tourism doesn't hurt the forests, the rivers, the sea, or the animals that live in them. Green tourists don't travel in big groups. They go around in small groups, so they don't disturb[6] the animals. And the tourist office asks people to take their trash with them when they leave.

Many tourists in Alaska take boat trips to see life in the sea. Whales are their favorite animal. The tourists go out on small boats and travel slowly and quietly. This way, they do not disturb the whales and the fish.

[6]**disturb:** make problems for people or animals

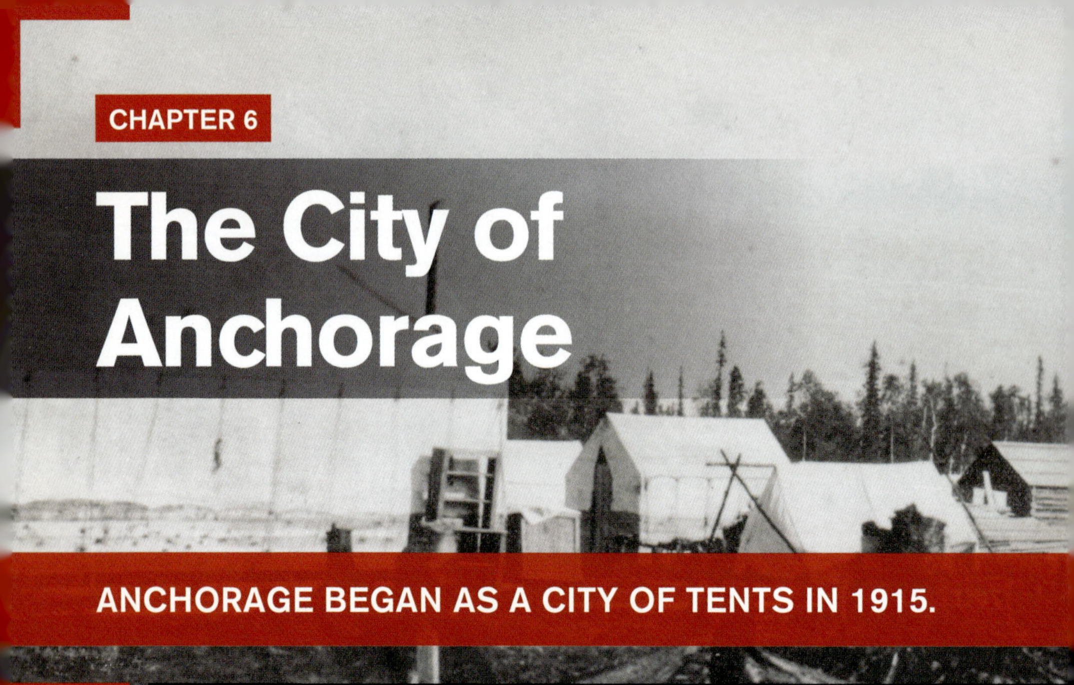

CHAPTER 6

The City of Anchorage

ANCHORAGE BEGAN AS A CITY OF TENTS IN 1915.

From 1915 to 1923, people went to live in Alaska to help build the railroad.[7] At that time, about 2,000 people lived in Anchorage. They all lived in tents, but only one tent had a bath in it!

By 1940, Anchorage had about 4,000 people, and in 2012, Anchorage was the biggest city in Alaska with 300,000 people. Anchorage is small, quiet, and pretty. Normally it's a safe place, too. But it wasn't on March 27, 1964.

Anchorage after the earthquake in 1964

That was a bad day in Anchorage. The ground under everyone's feet started to move. It didn't stop moving for four minutes. Houses fell and 115

[7] **railroad:** cars drive on roads and trains travel on a railroad

APPLY

Think about the town or city where you live. Do many people live there? Is it an old or a young city?

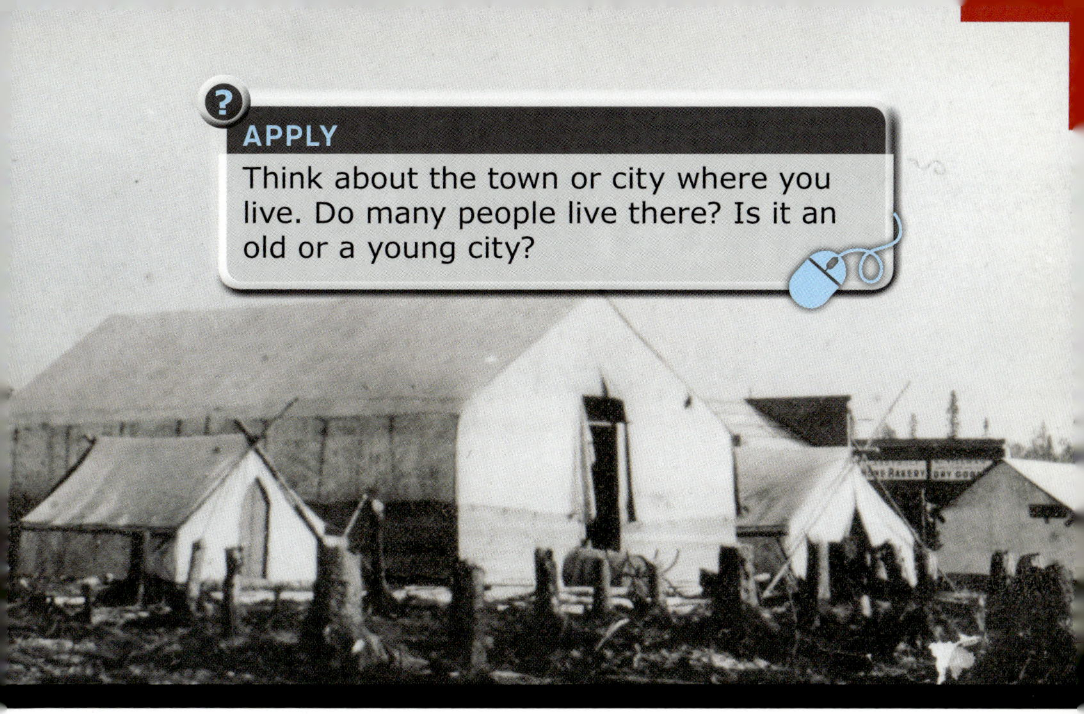

people died. It was an earthquake, a big earthquake, the second biggest earthquake in the world.

Today, Anchorage is an interesting city. During the day you can visit the Anchorage Museum. You can learn about the Eskimo people and life in the town many years ago. There are also many places to look at different kinds of art.[8] The H2Oasis Waterpark is a fun place to take children. And Kincaid Park is a good place to go to see animals.

At night you can go to a play at the theater, a concert, or out to dinner. Anchorage has some fantastic restaurants. Fish is the favorite of most people here, and many people say it is the best in the world.

---

[8] **art:** things such as paintings

CHAPTER 7

What Do You Think?

YOU ARE GOING WITH YOUR FAMILY TO VISIT ALASKA. THINK ABOUT WHAT YOU KNOW ABOUT ALASKA AND PLAN YOUR TRIP.

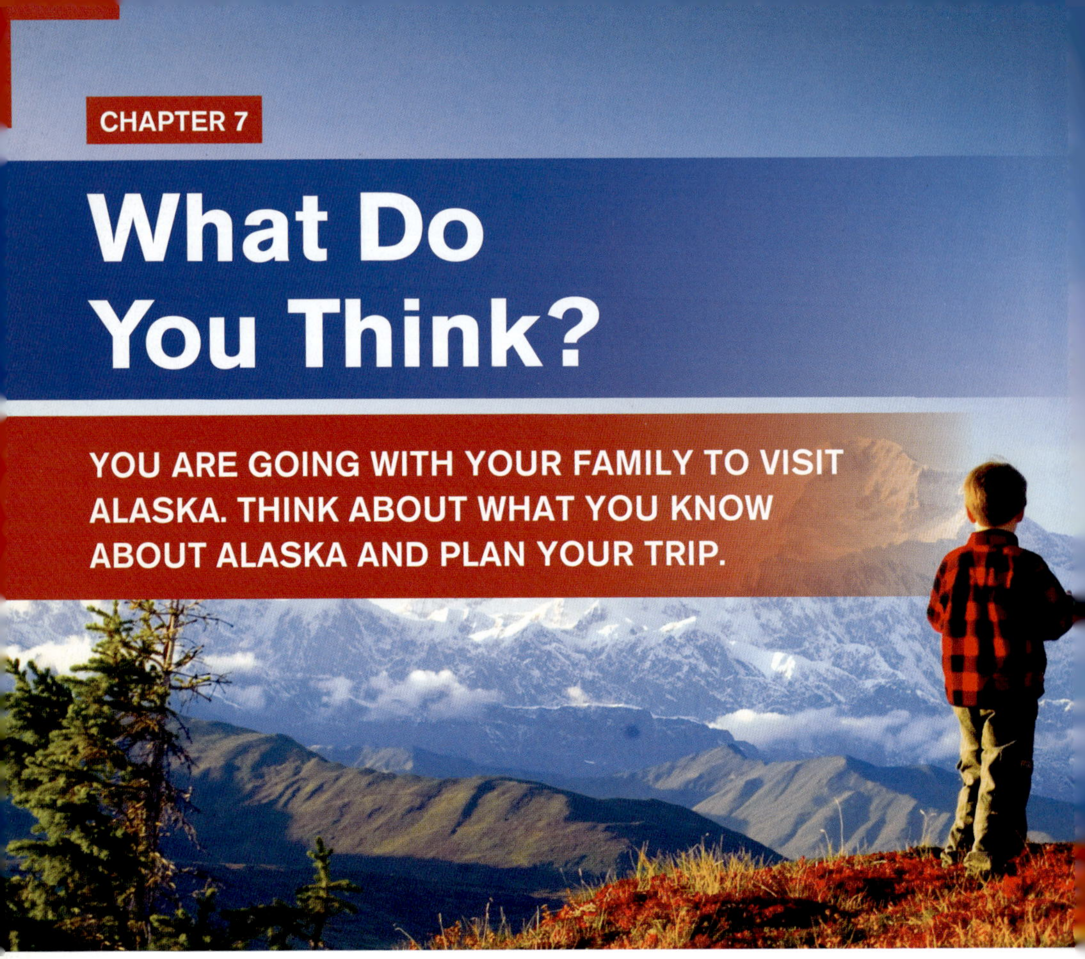

Answer these questions to help you plan your Alaska vacation.

- Would you like to stay in a tent, a hotel, or a house with an Alaskan family? Why?
- What clothes do you need to take for the weather in Alaska?
- On Kodiak Island would you like to go bear watching, paragliding, or mountain climbing? Which do you think is the most dangerous?

- Would you like to walk across Alaska, like Andrew Skurka? Do you think you can do it? What do you need to take with you?

- What kinds of green tourism do you want to try?

- Would you like to visit Anchorage? What would you like to do there?

- What would you like to buy to take home with you from Alaska? Some Alaskan fish? A jacket that the Eskimos wear? Some art from Kodiak Island?

Have a good trip!

After You Read

Choose the Correct Answers

Read the sentences and choose Ⓐ, Ⓑ, or Ⓒ.

1 The Inupiaq, the Yupik, and the Alutiiq people are different because ______

Ⓐ they don't eat the same food.
Ⓑ the Alutiiq are taller than the Yupik.
Ⓒ they don't speak the same language.

2 The people of Kodiak Island make their money from ______

Ⓐ the gold on the island.
Ⓑ the visitors to the island.
Ⓒ teaching English.

3 In 2012, four Japanese people died ______

Ⓐ climbing a mountain.
Ⓑ swimming in a river.
Ⓒ flying in a paraglider.

4 When Andrew Skurka travels, he ______

Ⓐ sleeps outside in a tent.
Ⓑ stays at a friend's house.
Ⓒ stays in a hotel.

5 Many Alaskan people think that the Iditarod is ______

Ⓐ a very boring race.
Ⓑ a very slow race.
Ⓒ an exciting race.

6 Places where green tourists go are ______

Ⓐ cleaner than other places.
Ⓑ noisier than other places.
Ⓒ more dangerous than other places.

7. The first people moved to Anchorage to ______
   - (A) work in the factories.
   - (B) make a railroad.
   - (C) start green tourism.

8. One day in 1964 was very bad for Anchorage because ______
   - (A) a lot of water came into the city.
   - (B) many people lost their lives.
   - (C) the temperature was –45°C.

Complete the Text

Use the words in the box to complete the e-mail from Andrew to his friend.

freezing	glacier	mountains	paragliding	race	tents

Hi, Jane!

I'm on vacation in Alaska with my family. I love it but the weather is very cold. Three days ago, we went camping in the forest. We slept in
1 ______________________ and it was fun. Then we went
2 ______________________. We flew over a beautiful
3 ______________________. It was 20 kilometers long, and all the ice moved very slowly.

There are many tall **4** ______________________ here, and people like to climb them. We saw the start of an exciting
5 ______________________ with people and dogs. They have to travel in **6** ______________________ weather.

See you soon!

Andrew

Answer Key

Words to Know, page 4

❶ forest ❷ paragliding ❸ tent ❹ snow storm ❺ Ice
❻ island

Words to Know, page 5

❶ freezing ❷ tourists ❸ dangerous ❹ popular ❺ climb
❻ mountain

Apply, page 7 *Answers will vary.*

Video Quest, page 9
The Kodiak bear is 3.35 meters tall when it stands up. It can eat more than 40 kilograms of food a day.

Video quest, page 11
You can see 100,000 glaciers from Mount Muir. A glacier can move 30 meters a day.

Evaluate, page 15 *Answers will vary.*

Video Quest, page 17
The Davidson Glacier is 14 kilometers long. It was 19 kilometers long at one time. When the world gets hotter, the ice melts.

Apply, page 19 *Answers will vary.*

Choose the Correct Answers, page 22

❶ C ❷ B ❸ A ❹ A ❺ C ❻ A ❼ B ❽ B

Complete the Text, page 23

❶ tents ❷ paragliding ❸ glacier ❹ mountains ❺ race
❻ freezing